Olivia Bennett

Rich World
Poor World

Macdonald

Acknowledgment

The author would like to thank all those who read and commented on the manuscript and in particular, the Information Department of ODA, the Aid Policy Research Group (FCO/ODA), the World Development Movement, R.R. Hodson of Manichur Community Development Project, Nepal, and Dr P. Moseley, Reader in Economics at Bath University.

A MACDONALD BOOK

First published in 1985 by
Macdonald & Co. (Publishers) Ltd
London and Sydney

© Olivia Bennett 1985

ISBN 0 356 10142 8

Macdonald & Co. (Publishers) Ltd
Maxwell House
74 Worship Street
London EC2A 2EN

A BPCC PLC company

Printed by Purnell & Sons (Book Production) Ltd
Paulton, near Bristol, Avon

BRITISH LIBRARY
CATALOGUING IN PUBLICATION DATA

Bennett, Olivia
    Rich world, poor world.—(Debates)
    1. Economic history—1971-
    I. Title   II. Series
    330.9′048   HC59

ISBN 0-356-10142-8

Contents

Rich world,

A critical discussion is currently taking place about the future of the world and its economy. The debate, also known as the North/South dialogue, is largely between two groups of countries: the so-called 'rich' and 'poor' countries.

A definition of terms Any division of the world into two such simple camps is bound to be inconsistent and arbitrary. Broadly speaking, however, countries in the poorer South include most of Asia, Africa and Latin America, China and parts of the Middle East. Most of these suffer from a low standard of living, high rate of population growth, and general economic and technological dependence on the rich world. They are known collectively as the South, the Third World, the poor world or developing countries, although none of these terms is universally accepted and all have their detractors.

Countries in the rich North include the whole of North America, Europe, the USSR, Japan, Australia and New Zealand. They used to be known as developed countries but that implied they had reached some 'ideal' level of development. Now the term industrialized countries is more common.

A further distinction is made within the rich world between the capitalist countries of western Europe, North America, Japan, New Zealand and Australia, and socialist countries, such as the USSR and those in eastern Europe. These are sometimes called the First and Second Worlds respectively.

How are countries classified as rich or poor? Their levels of wealth are often measured by their Gross National Product (GNP). This is the total value of goods and services (waged work) produced within a country. To that statisticians add all the payments received from other countries for exports and services, and deduct payments made to other countries for imports and services.

The issues Rich countries, which have become used to rapid improvements in living standards, now find themselves faced with recession, unemployment and inflation. Poor countries, which contain two-thirds of the world's population, are burdened with massive and spiralling debts and ever-increasing

Right Gross National Product can indicate the relative wealth of different countries.

Below Most people in the rich North live in comfortable homes with plenty to eat and every chance of getting the education and medical care they need.

Gross National Product *(All figures are in US dollars)*	
United Arab Emirates GNP *per capita*	28,110
Switzerland GNP *per capita*	15,980
United States GNP *per capita*	11,590
Great Britain GNP *per capita*	8,520
Singapore GNP *per capita*	4,420
Brazil GNP *per capita*	2,160
Somalia GNP *per capita*	260
Nepal GNP *per capita*	140

poor world?

numbers of people for whom hunger and poverty are a way of life. The poor world believes the international economic system works to its disadvantage, and is seeking ways to change it so that the system helps rather than hinders its economic development.

Conflicting fears and interests, both between and within the two groups, have led to endless discussion but little decision. Political and economic uncertainties and shifting circumstances make it hard, even for those most willing to change, to know exactly which proposals would decisively improve the situation. Indeed, the only thing on which everyone agrees is that the issues involved are extremely complex.

This book is an attempt to put forward some of the different points of view. It is not so much about answers as about questions – and the many conflicting sides to them. It is for you to

'Approximately 1,500 people die each day from lack of nourishment.'
Catholic Fund for Overseas Development

'The poor of the world must demand change . . . the only question at issue is whether the change comes by dialogue or confrontation.'
Julius Nyerere, President of Tanzania

find your own answers and form your own opinions. For, despite the grim facts about the poverty and hunger in the world, and the painfully slow progress towards effective action to eliminate them, people are still trying – in the firm belief that the solutions lie within our power.

The South contains two-thirds of the world's population and only one-fifth of its income. About 40 per cent of the people barely survive. In Calcutta alone, there are more than a quarter of a million pavement dwellers.

A question

The issues in the North/South debate are far from clearcut.

Problems of definition The neat division of the world into rich and poor, using convenient indicators of wealth such as GNP, is merely an attempt to clarify an extremely complex situation. In reality, things are not that simple. For example, it would be quite wrong to think of the poor world as a scene of unremitting poverty. Countries such as India and Brazil are becoming important industrial powers. Most of the oil-exporting countries are now very wealthy.

> 'The gap between rich and poor in the poor world is as great as it is between nations.'
> Geoffrey Lean, Rich World, Poor World

Right GNP figures can be misleading. Compare 'wealthy' Saudi Arabia's infant mortality rate with that of 'poor' Sri Lanka.

Below Not everyone in the poor world is poor. Most countries have a small wealthy élite, as here in the Philippines.

There is a huge variety of religious, cultural, social and political systems in the South, not to mention climates, terrain and available resources. As one economist put it: 'It is not possible to make many statements which could apply to India, Syria, the Central African Republic and Chile at the same time.' This complicates North/South negotiations, because the South's varied interests so often diverge and even conflict.

Within the rich world, too, there are divisions. The eastern bloc socialist countries support changes to the system which governs the world's economy, but are less willing to assist the poor world's development by the transfer of resources, whether of money, skills or equipment, because they feel they have never profited from the poor world through colonialism or commercial exploitation.

Similarly, the value of GNP statistics as a definitive measure of a country's wealth is questionable. For one thing, they don't indicate how evenly that wealth is distributed. There is as much inequality within the two worlds as between them. They also undervalue certain work, notably the considerable, unpaid contribution women make to food production. Perhaps more important and revealing indicators would be how healthy people are, how long they can expect to live, and whether they can go to school or college.

Infant Mortality Rate	
Sri Lanka	
GNP *per capita*	US $270
Infant mortality	1 in 27
Saudi Arabia	
GNP *per capita*	US $11,950
Infant mortality	1 in 9

How rich is rich? Other fundamental questions and assumptions underlie the whole discussion. Indeed, the very title of this book assumes some relative values. What do we mean by 'rich' and 'poor'? Someone on the dole in Britain is poor by UK standards but rich by those of a Bolivian peasant farmer. Can a distinction be made between the relative poverty of the unemployed in the UK, for example, supported by a welfare state, and the absolute poverty in which 800 million or more

# of values?

of the South's population live? Absolute poverty means having only the barest essentials of food, clothing and shelter.

There is also another kind of wealth, one which cannot be measured: the richness of a strong and supportive religious, cultural or social tradition. Some people feel the rich world has sacrificed its spiritual wealth for material growth. This raises the question of whether the rich world is a model worth imitating. Perhaps the debate should not be about how the poor world can catch up with the rich, but whether it should even try. Is there a better model for progress? Should the rich world start to question its pursuit of growth and the values which this entails? It may be that the two worlds have more to give to each other than economic concessions.

Certainly, as far as economics is concerned, many people feel that it is no longer a question of the rich 'aiding' the poor, but of both serving their mutual interests. In 1980 an international team of experts produced a report called *North:South, A Programme for Survival* (The Brandt Report). It stressed the interdependence of the modern world. Its theme was that

> '*Statistical measures of growth exclude the crucial elements of social welfare, of individual rights, of values not measurable by money.*'
>
> Brandt Report

North and South now share a common economic destiny, and that it is in everyone's interest to close the gap between the rich and poor and become one world.

Finally, there is the word 'development'. There has never been one definition that pleased everybody because people have different ideas about what is desirable progress. This is how the Brandt Report summed it up: 'Development is more than the passage from poor to rich, from a traditional rural economy to a sophisticated urban one. It carries with it not only the idea of economic betterment, but also of greater human dignity, security, justice and equity.' This book will be looking at the implications of this, and at the many problems which arise in attempting to achieve it.

Every so-called rich country also has its poor and disadvantaged.

Overpopulation –

A mother and child at a health clinic in Dominica, West Indies. Many of the world's poorer countries will, at their current rates of population growth, double their population in only 20 or 30 years. They'll need twice the number of schools, jobs, housing and food supplies just to maintain their present standard of living.

problem or myth?

Probably one of the most widely held views about Third World countries is that they are poor because they are overpopulated. Population growth has been called 'an even more subtle and dangerous threat to the world than thermonuclear war'. Apart from fears of social and political unrest caused by increasing numbers of people whom governments can neither feed, house nor employ, high birthrates also fuel the belief that much development aid is wasted, since any progress is immediately cancelled out by the rise in population.

Development – the best contraceptive?
Many poor women simply don't have access to contraceptive help. Some face opposition, or at least disinterest from men, in controlling the number of children they have. Clearly, there is a need for more effective family planning services. However, while some believe that there's no real chance of improving the living standards of the poor until population growth slows down, others argue that a better standard of living would in itself bring about lower birthrates.

Poor people are not having large families because they are irresponsible, they say, but because they live in a poor country with a rudimentary welfare state and therefore see children as security against a destitute old age. They argue that families scratching a living from the land need all the helping hands they can get, and that couples have many babies because not all will survive. In some poor countries, as many as one in four children die before their first birthday. It can take several generations before parents really trust in reduced levels of infant mortality and plan their families accordingly.

There is therefore an argument for not tackling population growth in isolation, but seeing a reduction as going with or following an improvement in living standards. In South Korea and Taiwan, for example, lower birthrates have coincided with the sort of improved social and economic conditions which help reduce people's need for children, as wage-earners or labourers.

Yet many regard the theory that higher incomes and standards of health and education automatically bring about lower birthrates as dangerously oversimplified. They believe the relationship between poverty and large families is more complicated. In Kenya, they point out, there has also been considerable economic development, yet its population is growing faster than before. This is in spite of the fact that most of the people live off the land, and that each generation is finding itself with less and less land on which to grow food, as parents divide their farms between their children. To ignore the crucial role played by unplanned population growth is, they believe, irresponsible and simplistic.

Overpopulation may not be the *cause* of poverty, and better living standards *can* have a beneficial effect on population growth. However, it would be hard to deny the enormous burden that the doubling of a poor country's population in just 30 years places on its ability simply to maintain existing standards of living, let alone improve them and provide the extra school places, homes, jobs, food and water supplies required.

'If we don't have children, will you *look after* us when we're ill or old?' *Peruvian peasant farmer*

'More than 200,000 additional faces appear at the world's breakfast table every day.' *Population Concern*

'Population growth can aggravate hunger but it doesn't cause it.' *Food for Beginners*

The colonial

Europeans' prime motive for colonization was to exploit the natural resources of the colonies and gain raw materials for their industries; to expand their own markets for manufactured goods; and to use the plentiful supplies of land and labour to grow the crops they needed. While critics admit that many who served in the colonies sincerely wished to help, they maintain that the systems they imposed often had the opposite effect.

In many colonies the European administration persuaded local people to change from growing food crops to growing the cash crops the colonial powers wanted (such as cotton, rubber or sugar). This reduced their self-sufficiency and left them vulnerable to food shortages. There had been times of drought and low productivity before but, with so much of their land given over to cash crops, people no longer had the resources to survive them.

The colonial legacy By selling their own manufactured goods, the colonialists destroyed some traditional industries, such as the Indian textile business. They left many countries with economies dependent on just one or two exports. This means that these countries are very vulnerable to price fluctuations in the world market for their goods.

To some people the country boundaries themselves are one of the most damaging of colonial legacies, since they were often imposed by the European powers on the basis of their own political considerations, and not on ethnic, regional or historical ones. These arbitrary boundaries have been blamed for much of the political instability and civil wars that have plagued some Third World countries since independence.

Many smaller countries would benefit from greater cooperation with their neighbours, yet colonial history has linked poorer countries with richer ones rather than with each other, particularly in trade and communications. The rich have the capital, expertise and equipment the poor need, and are their main markets.

An incomplete picture? However, while colonialism may be one reason why poor countries are poor, it cannot be considered the whole answer. There are plenty of examples to show that being an ex-colony does not automatically mean being poor. Australia is an ex-colony and is rich. Ghana and Tanzania are ex-colonies and poor – some would argue poorer since independence. Nepal is even poorer and was never colonized. Singapore was a colony and is rich and industrialized.

In many cases, the colonial powers provided a sound infrastructure, for example roads, railways, bridges and ports. These represent considerable financial and technical investment. They did the initial prospecting for minerals and other raw materials, and established plantations and mines which are still valuable. It may not be ideal to be dependent on one or two exports, but it is better than having none at all.

The colonialists also left an educational and judicial framework which at least gave the newly independent countries something to modify. Some people would argue, however, that modern versions of these countries' tradi-

A sugar plantation in the West Indies, 1876. Many ex-colonies say that the problems they have now in feeding themselves are the fault of their former masters, who set a pattern of using the best land to grow cash crops for export, rather than food for the local population.

connection

tional social systems would have been better. The imposition of western ideas has, they feel, done harm by eroding traditional values and culture. In addition, the adoption of western models of education and health care has led to systems which serve a minority well rather than the majority adequately.

'Colonial rule generally promoted material advance, especially a rise in living standards.' *Professor Bauer,* Dissent on Development

A fine bronze head from Benin, West Africa. All three continents of the Third World have had powerful, wealthy and highly sophisticated civilizations. To many, the loss of traditional cultural and social systems is the most damaging result of colonial rule.

'Without exception [the imperialists] left us nothing but our resentment.' *Kwame Nkrumah, ex-President of Ghana*

Inevitable

Some people feel that hunger and poverty are inevitable in developing countries, which they see as constantly plagued by floods, droughts and other problems. This view of the poor world as a collection of countries hopelessly vulnerable to natural disasters (and man-made ones, too, such as war) is well-served by the western media, for whom a disaster is news while quiet unremarkable progress is not. Some charities, too, have overstressed the helplessness of the poor world in order to raise funds, although most are now changing this approach.

Are the poor disaster-prone? It is true that most poor countries lie in the tropics. Rainfall there is often erratic and water supplies scarce (which affects both food production and health). Some lack natural resources, or those they have are very difficult to exploit and require more money or expertise than is available. Others have inhospitable terrain which hampers communication and development. Some lie in the hurricane or earthquake belts.

> '*A hostile natural environment has been one of the key restraints in holding back economic development.*'
>
> Paul Harrison, Inside the Third World

However, it is also people's very poverty which makes them particularly vulnerable to natural disasters. Rich countries are affected by hurricanes and tornadoes, too. But cheap structures collapse more easily, and poor countries lack elaborate welfare systems to help the victims. Similarly, properly irrigated and drained land can cope with floods, where a poor farmer may find everything he has invested in the soil swept away. A Red Cross report found that, in the West, the average disaster death toll was 500; in the Third World

disaster?

it was 3,000. Poverty, it concluded, was the real killer.

The poor have least resistance to disasters, while the rich can survive and even exploit them. Farmers who are only just managing to eke out a living from the soil can be devastated by a period of low rainfall. For the rich farmer with crops in store, a famine can be profitable as food prices rise and his stored grain becomes in greater demand.

Money and expertise can go a long way towards solving problems of environment. Europe's mountainous regions are well-served by road, rail and air. Not so the land-locked, mountainous regions of the poor world. Holland is low-lying, and prone to flooding, yet rich because it has had the resources to use its land to best advantage.

Man-made problems Environmentalists point out that many 'inhospitable' terrains in the poor world have been successfully farmed by generations of people. Farmers terraced steep hillsides. Nomadic herders survived in the apparently hostile desert.

Left The aftermath of a hurricane in Andhra Pradesh, India. Extreme weather conditions are just one of the problems many poor countries have to contend with. Their poverty increases their vulnerability, for flimsy housing and rudimentary infrastructure are easily destroyed.

> 'The sun shines and the rain falls differently on different social strata.'
>
> Food for Beginners

In recent years, however, the balance between people and nature has suffered. Desertification is increasing alarmingly. Deforestation is a major problem in many poor countries and is causing dramatic soil erosion and flooding.

Much of this is due to greatly increased pressure of population. Some of it, however, is because peasants have been pushed off the most productive land by companies wanting to grow cash crops, and forced to retreat onto hillsides or into forests. They have little choice there but to 'over'-cultivate or 'over'-graze. And so their poverty aggravates their problems.

Who's to

A young electrical engineer being trained in Chile. There is no shortage of people with the will to learn in the poor world, but the lack of training opportunities is a major constraint to development.

Some say that poverty is largely people's 'own fault', claiming that the poor are lazy, or lack ambition, or spend what money they have unwisely. Peasant families, for example, have been criticised for spending their savings on weddings and funerals, sometimes to the extent of losing their only productive asset: their land. Others complain that the poor are passive and unwilling to change.

However, many would argue that the peasant farmer is not against change *per se*, but point out that it is naive to expect people on the edge of starvation to risk new agricultural methods unless they feel confident of their success. Years of poverty breed fatalism, not the other way around. And, most seriously, tropical climates and persistent ill-health caused by malnourishment and impure water supplies are a continuous drain on the poor's strength and energy.

Different values? A common criticism of the Third World is the existence there of widespread corruption. Government bureaucrats, in particular, are often accused of being less interested in national goals than in regional, ethnic or simply personal ones. Corruption is a major problem in many countries, but criticisms by westerners can sometimes stem from a lack of understanding of social and cultural traditions which have their own strengths.

What one person calls corruption or nepotism may be acceptable within a social system which places looking after one's family high on the list of moral duties. Indeed, some people in the rich world now look with respect and envy at the mutual supportiveness of some poorer communities, particularly the extended family unit. And it should be remembered that poor countries often pay their government em-

blame?

ployees very little. Creating a system of un-official perks may be the only way to get a living wage.

Are governments to blame? It is generally recognized that the main problems of the poor world are not so much a lack of energy or ambition as a shortage of skills, and a failure of key institutions to formulate and follow appropriate policies. Many poor countries reply to such criticisms by pointing out the difficulty they have in forecasting in the short-term, let alone planning in the long-term, when their economies depend on selling one or two commodities, the prices of which may fluctu-ate dramatically. Thus, they say, their attempts at development are constantly thwarted by economic factors over which they have no control.

However, it would seem, too, that the ruling élite in the Third World have often been more interested in imitating the rich world than in searching for workable models more appropriate to the needs of their people. Sometimes encouraged by western influence and advice, they have formulated over-ambi-tious and inconsistent plans, occasionally based on incomplete or unreliable statistical data. Research requires money and skilled personnel; poor countries may lack both.

Many argue that poor countries can achieve little until rich ones have the political will to share the world's resources more equally. But it is perhaps equally important for this will to develop on the part of the rich and powerful within the poor world itself. Without their willingness to share resources more equitably and to follow more appropriate models of development, the poorest in the poor world have little chance of progress.

'You don't make poor people richer by making their government richer' Oxfam

All too often, prestige developments in the Third World, such as these skyscrapers in Calcutta, are not accompanied by comparable improvements in conditions for the very poor.

The trade trap

Opposite Picking out waste matter from drying cocoa beans in Grenada, West Indies. Many poor countries supply the raw materials for the rich world's food and manufacturing industries. The prices of these commodities are fixed in the markets of the rich world and are often both too low and unstable.

While virtually no countries today remain colonies in the political sense, many feel that economic colonialism is alive and kicking. Many developing countries remain only suppliers of raw materials and primary products. Moreover, more than half of them are dependent on one or two crops or minerals (excluding oil), and some obtain almost all their export earnings from one product, for example Zambia (copper) and Mauritius (sugar). A few are rapidly industrializing (eg. Singapore, Hong Kong and Brazil), but the South's share of the world's trade in manufactured goods is still only 10 per cent of the total (while it has 70 per cent of the world's population).

The prices that commodities fetch are determined in rich country commodity markets and are vulnerable to speculation and fluctuation. Moreover, nearly all the processing, packaging and marketing of these products, such as turning coffee beans into 'instant' coffee, is done in the industrialized countries—and this is where most of the profit lies.

> **'Without exception there is an adverse balance of trade with former rulers.'**
> Agribusiness in Africa

The need for stability Poor countries not only claim that the prices paid for their raw materials are too low; they also complain that they are unstable. The prices of fuel oil and manufactured goods have steadily risen. Twenty-five tonnes of rubber, which bought six tractors in 1960, bought only two tractors in 1975. Oil price rises in the 1970s, and inflation and recession in the rich world, have made the situation much worse. Commodity prices have not followed the consistent rise in the price of manufactured goods but have shot up and down erratically, upsetting the best laid plans of poor countries for economic progress. Some poor country raw materials are also under threat from man-made substitutes and synthetics.

All these factors place poor countries in a weak position which, they claim, merely adds to their troubles by sometimes forcing them to sell when the market is at its worst for them. They want agreements to raise and stabilize commodity prices, and a greater share of the employment and profits from manufacturing and processing.

Is change feasible? The North argues the difficulty of meeting these demands, saying that if the South wants to distort the market and interfere with the workings of free trade by forcing artificially high prices for its goods, it simply won't get customers. And if someone invents a nylon rope which does a better job than sisal rope, it is naive to say that it's part of a conspiracy by the North against the South: the world has to learn to cope with change or simply stagnate.

But poor countries ask why, if change is a good thing, is the rich world so resistant to cheaper imports from the South which would allow it to alter the balance of trade and increase its share of the world's industry?

There is some debate as to whether, over the long term, world trade has been so unfavourable to commodity producers. It is very hard to quantify. Certainly there have been periods in the past when the terms of trade have favoured commodity producers, and some economists believe such a period may be on the way again. However, most would agree that for some time now the situation has not been a happy one for most countries dependent on exports of raw materials. So recent debate has centred not so much on whether there is a need to stabilize and raise prices, but on how to do it.

'In 1963 we needed to produce 5 tons of sisal to buy a tractor. In 1970 we had to produce 10 tons of sisal to buy that same tractor.'

President Nyerere of Tanzania

Narrowing

The export of commodities (of which 75 per cent are raw and unprocessed) is the Third World's most important source of foreign exchange. Earnings from such exports amounted to more than 10 times all the aid received, for example, in 1982. So, for the poor world, an improvement in commodity prices would be a crucial step in the bid to narrow the gap between them and the rich.

A New International Economic Order? In a series of conferences since the early 1970s, the poorer countries have been pressing for changes which, after 1974, became known as the 'New International Economic Order' (NIEO). They have called for more stable prices, linked to the price of manufactured goods, more opportunities to process their own raw materials, and greater access to markets in which to sell them.

The ways and means to achieve a fairer international trade system are debated at meetings of the United Nations Conference on Trade and Development (UNCTAD). One of

Jute mill, Bangladesh. Poor countries not ony want higher and more stable prices for their goods but also a greater share in the manufacturing and processing of them, which is where most of the profit lies.

'*Underdevelopment is about lack of power.*'
World Development Movement

the gap?

the proposals discussed is to stabilize the swings in commodity prices by building up buffer stocks, so that supplies can be drawn on at times of low productivity and stocks bought at times of surplus. This should protect prices from erratic rise and fall. But some commodities (eg. bananas) can't be stored. Some, in order to fight the challenge of a synthetic substitute, may have to agree to lower prices. Others, where the price is continually falling, may find the buffer stock has quickly turned into a mountain.

In some cases, the only real help would be some sort of compensation when export earnings drop below a certain level. This is being attempted through a scheme called Stabex. Poor countries would also like the prices of their exports to be linked to those of the manufactured imports they need, so that they could plan ahead more realistically. Many rich countries have not supported this demand, saying it is simply a recipe for continued world inflation.

Problems and pitfalls The establishment of a Common Fund to finance buffer stocks and other arrangements for commodities are constantly being debated.

The rich world has been prepared to study ways of stabilizing the export earnings of the poor world, but has not always reached the same conclusions as poor countries. It feels that the commodities are so different that they should be considered separately. The South, on the other hand, wants an overall framework for the agreements, and the money to make them work, before it considers the details on individual commodities, many of which it feels should not be considered in isolation.

Some people fear that demands for higher, more stable prices will not really help the poorest. Higher prices for cash crops will merely entrench their production and thus the dominant rich élite who profit from them. They say poor countries should concentrate on increasing their self-reliance and developing economic cooperation between each other, while at the same time pressing for much more power at the decision-making levels of international trade and finance.

Many Third World countries want to protect themselves from the situation of finding that western countries have decided to lower inflation by raising interest rates, so that the poor world has to pay more for its loans, and thus pay the price of rich world inflation.

Jobs

Changing the world pattern of manufacture, pricing and selling is called 'restructuring'. One of the elements of restructuring most often discussed is the South's desire to increase its share of the world's manufacturing, and of the markets in which to sell manufactured products.

Protectionism People in the North fear that, if the South starts manufacturing more of its own goods and competing with them, it will lead to massive unemployment. And western governments have to consider the needs and opinions of the people who elect them or they lose votes.

One way they have responded to these fears is to set up tariff and other barriers which protect national industries from foreign competition. Heavy taxes on imports, for example, make them more expensive than home-produced goods. This is called 'protectionism'. Third World countries have done the same when their plans for industrialization meant replacing foreign imports with local goods.

Many feel that protectionism is an expensive way of keeping industries going which may no longer have a future in the North, such as the steel or textile industries. Postponing restructuring can make the effects of it much worse when it finally comes. However, protectionism can be a help when it is used to buy time – time in which industries can change and people can learn new skills in occupations that do have a future in the North, such as, perhaps, research, engineering, computing or other high technology areas.

It should be recognized that those in the North most likely to suffer from unemployment are the poorest and most vulnerable in society – immigrants, women and the unskilled. Efforts on the part of unions and governments to protect them are therefore understandable. But poor countries put this into perspective by pointing out that at least

> 'It is true we have taken protectionist measures against the import of textiles . . . we have to take into consideration the opinion of our people.'
>
> *Olaf Palme, Prime Minister of Sweden*

Manufacturing trousers in Poona, India. Some industries in the North have declined because of competition from the South, but far more jobs are lost because of new technology.

in jeopardy?

these people have the benefit of social security. Most Third World workers have no such benefit to cushion the impact of unemployment.

With unemployment in industrialized countries on the increase, it is not surprising that feelings on this issue run high. Yet what exactly are the major challenges to jobs in the North? Government studies have shown that in Britain, for example, the main competition to UK goods comes from other rich countries, such as Japan, the USA and EEC countries. In fact, an increased Third World demand for certain goods which require British technical skills and machinery would actually create new jobs. Of course, some jobs are lost through competition from the South, but the same studies showed that 4½ times as many were lost because of new technology.

Interdependence? For practically every category of manufacture, the North sells far more to the South than it buys back, so it has a lot of valuable trade to lose.

> 'In Britain, between 1960 and 1970 manufactured goods from the Third World displaced less than 2% of the workforce.'
> *Catholic Fund for Overseas Development*

Some people believe that there is no danger in the South increasing its share of manufacturing, provided the North can at the same time create new jobs and markets. More recession in the West, they say, won't profit anyone, rich or poor; whereas if the overall market increases worldwide, then everyone prospers.

Yet, of course, if the world market really is to increase, then the South has to become better off so that the poor begin to have real spending power and can actually buy manufactured goods. As the Brandt Report put it: 'The North cannot prosper ... unless there is greater progress in the South.'

Queueing for unemployment benefit in Florida, USA. Many people in the North fear that jobs will be lost if the South starts manufacturing its own goods.

Slow

Right Supermarket shelves groan under the weight of luxury imported goods. Yet many of the foodstuffs we buy are grown in Third World countries whose population goes hungry.

The United Nations Conference on Trade and Development (UNCTAD), which meets about every four years, is the traditional forum for the North/South dialogue. What goes on at these meetings is thus a barometer of the state of the debate. After the sixth UNCTAD, in 1983, many feared the conference had reached stalemate.

Who's to blame? The poor world accuses the rich of resisting any really effective restructuring, and of paying little more than lip-service to its demands. Some feel the North's policy is just to 'keep them talking' for as long as possible, so that nothing is actually done.

The North claims it is not unwilling to respond to the South's demands, but that the developing countries have not yet produced a workable alternative to the present system. They also argue that the inflexibility of the South leaves little room for negotiation.

The South accuses the North of only responding passively to proposals, rather than coming up with constructive ones of its own. It was the countries of the South, they say, who got the UN General Assembly to accept a

programme of action for the New International Economic Order (NIEO), yet they feel their attempts to implement it have been blocked at every turn by the rich countries.

Divergence of interests? Certainly, one of the difficulties for the poor world is that it is made up of countries seeking many different answers to a wide variety of needs. Their interests are not at all the same: for example, Nigeria wants a high oil price, its neighbour Ghana wants a low one. And, apart from oil, the raw materials which they have to use as bargaining tools are either not vital to the world economy (eg. bananas or coffee) or they don't have a monopoly over their export (eg. tin or copper).

Most of their products have a limited market, so the producers have to compete for their share of it, rather than act together. Oil producers, with the huge world market, were the exceptions. It is significant that the first time bargaining power was in the hands of a group of primary producers was when the Organization of Petroleum Exporting Countries (OPEC) increased the price of oil in 1973. But the oil

> 'The South has got to reach beyond governments [of the North] and help convert the people.'
> *Shridath Ramphal, Commonwealth Secretary-General*

> 'Redistribution within countries is just as important . . . as between them.'
> *Geoffrey Lean, Rich World, Poor World*

> 'Lack of progress at international trade conferences could turn out to be the death knell of future co-operation.'
> *Christian Aid*

progress?

situation changed too quickly for this position of strength to last.

Self-interest? Some people believe that the North/South dialogue is not about how best to help the poor, but simply a fight about power.

Frustrated by the slow progress of the dialogue – caused, as they see it, by the fact that national self-interest is the only real driving force behind negotiations between and within the international community – they believe that attempts to move rich countries on moral grounds are less productive than appeals directed to self-interest alone. They stress that the rich world is not being asked to make sacrifices or give anything up, because

ultimately it can only gain from a more prosperous South. They argue that the world is now so interdependent that the achievement of economic growth in one country, or group of countries, cannot be separated from growth in others.

Yet, as long as the people who elect western governments see concessions to the South as resulting in reductions in their own standard of living, are their governments going seriously to consider proposals which are likely to lose them votes? This is why some feel that a first crucial step is to get ordinary people to recognize that their economic interests are intimately bound up with those of poor countries.

Working on an oil rig in Saudi Arabia. In the early 1970s the oil-exporting countries were the first primary producers effectively to combine to ask a higher price for their commodity. But fluctuating demand has undermined even their position.

The UN –

The slow progress of the North/South debate has also been blamed on the fact that the major institutions set up to promote change – such as the various United Nations organizations – are simply inadequate. Indeed, by giving the rich world the means to keep the poor world talking for as long as possible, some say the UN system has done more harm than good. It actually forestalls effective change, they argue, by giving the appearance of progress without the reality.

How useful is the UN? UN officials are often criticised for believing that if they draft enough high-sounding resolutions the job is half-done, when it has not even been effectively started. Others say that the real arena of change and discussion is now outside the UN – as, for example, when certain international debt problems forced rich world governments and banks to work out solutions with the poor world.

Yet it is also said that by the time the various groups meet at for example, UNCTAD, they are so firmly set in their positions that there is no room for manoeuvre. In other words, it is not so much the UN which is at fault as the way member countries use it.

Aid organizations In addition to giving the poor world a voice in international affairs through the General Assembly, the UN provides the umbrella under which many organizations disperse aid and research development strategies. Not everyone feels the same about their effectiveness.

Some say the UN multilateral agencies (which distribute funds on behalf of groups of countries) are good because they reduce the possibility of individual countries using aid as

> 'What has happened is that governments have failed to use the UN system properly.'
>
> Shridath Ramphal,
> Commonwealth
> Secretary-General

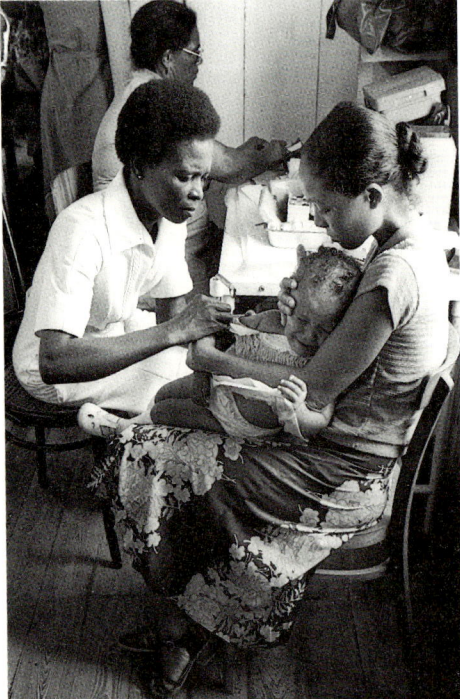

A World Health Organization vaccination programme against measles, which kills or disables millions of children every year. The UN's specialized agencies have the benefit of international expertise, but have been criticised for inefficiency and waste.

UN organizations

FAO – Food and Agriculture
Organization
IBRD – International Bank for
Reconstruction and Development
(World Bank)
IMF – International Monetary Fund
UNCTAD – United Nations Conference
on Trade and Development
UNDRO – United Nations Disaster
Relief Office
UNDP – United Nations Development
Programme
UNESCO – United Nations Educational,
Scientific and Cultural Organization
UNEP – United Nations Environment
Programme
UNFPA – United Nations Fund for
Population Activities
UNICEF – United Nations Children's Fund
WHO – World Health Organization

friend or foe?

a bargaining tool for political ends. They also reduce the possibility of donor countries competing with each other for the most prestigious projects (which are not necessarily the most beneficial to the poor), or of duplicating aspects of each other's work through lack of communication.

The counter argument is that multilateral agencies are themselves quite capable of duplication and inadequate consultation. At times they even work in opposition. For example, the WHO spends money on anti-smoking measures, while the FAO funds tobacco-growing projects. The most frequent criticism is that the agencies suffer from a dangerous lack of accountability, and an unacceptably high ratio of administrative costs to effective action.

Many rich and poor countries have traditional links which can assist development cooperation, and this mutually beneficial relationship is lost in the anonymity of multilateral organizations. However, bilateral aid (from one government directly to another), while in theory more accountable to taxpayers, is not necessarily better or more carefully administered, and can be affected by conflicting commercial or political considerations.

> 'The UN at least created a political framework within which small countries begin to have a voice.'
>
> Michael Manley, ex-Prime Minister of Jamaica

The mistakes made by all large aid organizations are now generally recognized, and lessons are being drawn from them. However, many feel that small, non-governmental organizations (charities like Oxfam, for example) are much more effective at getting aid to the very poor – those who need it most.

The United Nations General Assembly. Nations of the South outnumber and so can outvote the nations of the North. Critics of the UN say it does the South more harm than good, by encouraging talk rather than action.

The money market

All countries engaged in world trade are affected by events in the world monetary system. After the end of the Second World War, that system tried to prevent a repetition of the 1930s depression and was centred on the International Monetary Fund (IMF). For about 25 years there was considerable economic stability, and living standards in the industrialized countries rose consistently.

In the early 1970s a number of aspects of the system broke down, and the world's monetary and economic relations have been increasingly strained ever since. Developing countries, which had been borrowing money to fund economic growth, found that the end of the boom in the rich world brought a collapse in the prices paid for their products, making it difficult for them to repay their loans. At the same time as the markets for their exports shrank, the interest payments on their loans rose as the industrialized countries tried to control inflation by increasing interest rates.

The collective debt of the poor world was estimated at over $800 billion in 1984, and grows every year. Much of the debt is concentrated in Latin America and particularly in Brazil, Argentina and Mexico, in other words not the poorest countries in the Third World. Probably the most frustrating part of the debt crisis is that the huge sums of money involved are not being productively invested but simply being recycled between banks.

Much of the indignation of the poor world about their dependence on the rich stems from this feeling that they are victims of circumstances over which they have little or no control. In the case of their debt burden, it is fair to say that much of the problem is due to developments in the rich world, particularly the high interest rates.

The International Monetary Fund Many developing countries feel critical of the IMF, created to lend money to countries in financial difficulties where banks were reluctant to help. Some Third World countries have been annoyed because the IMF has seemed to imply that their difficulties are their own fault, rather than being brought about by the behaviour of banks or governments in the rich world.

Like any banker, the IMF needs to satisfy itself that the borrower will be able to repay its loan. The money is only lent after the IMF has scrutinized a country's economy and laid down specific conditions as to how it should be run in the future. Critics say the IMF imposes conditions which take a short-term view of a country's problems, and which may ignore or distort its long-term aims over the kind of development it wishes to pursue. They feel the IMF never looks at things from a Third World point of view, and applies the sort of prescriptions which may work in a developed industrialized society but be inappropriate in a poor country.

Yet no poor country is obliged to go to the IMF for help, and it can be argued that if a country does want financial aid, then it is only fair for the lender to ask the borrower to follow policies which it believes will strengthen its economy and allow it to pay off its debts.

Unpopular with the people? One of the problems is that many of the IMF policies, however necessary, are very unpopular. They may cause social unrest as when, for example, the IMF says to hold down wages, cut back social services, raise food prices and pay more to farmers to stimulate production.

Some governments' objection to IMF reforms may be as much because they threaten their power and popularity as because they actually hurt the poorest. It is argued that the IMF has even proved a useful scapegoat for some governments, who could blame it for enforcing necessary correctives which they themselves were unwilling to be seen to impose.

'The IMF is not responding to the real needs of the international community.'

Shridath Ramphal, Commonwealth Secretary-General

'It is necessary and legitimate for the IMF to lay down conditions for the members who borrow from it.'

Brandt Report

Big

Developing countries obtain finance from a number of sources. As well as international institutions such as the IMF, the World Bank, the regional development banks and UN organizations, there are commercial banks, government-to-government aid programmes, and private investment. Much of the latter comes from multinational companies, which are themselves a source of debate and controversy. The size of their operations means that they touch the lives of people all over the globe, even in the most remote and poorest areas.

Transnational companies Many people prefer the word 'transnational' to 'multinational', because it stresses an important feature of these companies – the movement of money across and between nations. Multinational makes it sound as if several countries are equal partners in the company, whereas in fact what happens is that the company may have factories and offices in many countries but its roots and shareholders are usually in only one or two, most commonly the USA or a European country.

> 'There is no better way to harness man's self-interest than through the competitive market economy.'
> C.F. Sedcole, Unilever PLC

The good side? Transnational companies provide jobs and pay taxes which help support, for example, the host country's social services. Their direct investment, unlike official loans, can help poor countries without saddling them with additional debts. They train and build up local manpower skills at all levels – technical and managerial. Their employees may save and invest money, which can lead to further productive investment and increased spending power. A company may also stimulate other small industries because of the demand it generates for certain products and services.

The bad side? Transnational companies may stifle local competition or put smaller, weaker operations out of business. They can absorb scarce facilities which would otherwise go to home-grown industries. They sometimes ensure that a very large proportion of the profits goes back to the parent company in the rich world. They may keep their technical skills to themselves and only employ and train nationals in the lower levels of the workforce, reserving all the top management jobs for expatriates.

business

Because of their transnational nature, they will look at the development of an industry in a poor country in terms of its benefit to the parent company, not to the poor country itself. Some may be large and powerful enough to influence governments and local political affairs. Codes of practice have been formulated to try and prevent such practices, and among other things to compel big corporations to invest more of their profits locally.

Many poor country governments have actively encouraged big business, wanting to attract foreign investment as part of their programme of industrialization. Others oppose private investment in any form, saying

'In many ways the large multinational companies are the new colonialists of our day.'

Christian Aid

that development which depends on profit-making and entrepreneurship outside the control of the state can only widen the gap between rich and poor. Their opponents reply that, in practice, this means state controls, excessive bureaucracy and inadequate rewards, which in turn often stifle local production and encourage corruption.

This Pepsi-Cola bottling plant is one of several factories in remote North Yemen owned by foreign companies. Many poor countries want foreign investment; but they may not always see much of the profits, and the products themselves may be inappropriate.

'A vigorous aid policy is an investment in a healthier world economy.'
Brandt Report

The role of aid?

There are a variety of different sources which developing countries can tap for finance. However, the very poor countries have not been able to raise much money on commercial terms. For them, aid is the principal source of funds.

Given freely? Although aid has been increasing over the years, inflation has caused it to fall in value in real terms. Rich countries have, with very few exceptions, not reached the UN's target of giving 0.7 per cent of their GNP to aid.

In addition, a good deal of the aid is given not as a gift but as a loan. Much aid is 'tied', which means the recipient has to use it to buy goods and services from the donor. Some argue that this has the double benefit of stimulating jobs in the donor country, and trade between rich and poor. But it also means the poor country has no choice over the supplier and the type of goods and services, which might have been available locally, or even their price. Even aid which is given without conditions attached often goes back in part to the rich countries in the form of salaries for 'experts', equipment bought, and so on.

A great deal of aid is given each year, and the Brandt Report called for it to be increased, in spite of the fact that many rich countries are suffering the effects of recession and are not in the mood to maintain, let alone increase payments.

Yet aid has its opponents, too, in both rich and poor worlds. As the journalist Geoffrey Lean points out, much of the poor world's 'sense of grievance is not about a lack of money; it is about a lack of dignity and independence.' Many poor countries don't want favours or acts of charity; they want the chance to control their own destinies and not to be at the mercy of an economic system which they have so little power to influence. To them aid smacks of dependence, and they reject any proposals which seem to mean aid in another form. They want nothing less than a wholesale restructuring of the international economic order.

Charity begins at home? There are those in the North who insist that their aid programmes are already too generous, and that the world recession means that even rich countries do not have the money to spare. Others claim that there simply aren't the resources in the world to cope with its huge population; this is sometimes called the 'lifeboat' theory. The rich countries are in a lifeboat floating on a sea in which everyone else is starving. If they pull in the 'starving millions', the boat will overturn and *everyone* will drown. Some just feel that aid never reaches the poorest.

> '*Charity corrupts giver and taker alike, and only increases poverty.*' F. Dostoievsky, The Possessed

Supporters of aid argue the case for it on a number of grounds. There are those who feel that ex-colonial powers have an obligation to repay some of the wealth they extracted. Others feel that the rich have a moral duty to assist the poor as part of humanity.

Many experts point out how interdependent the world's nations have become, warning that the rich ignore the plight of the world's poor at their peril. The rich world needs political allies in the South, and development cooperation is a way of fostering political friendships – and trading relationships, too, for the industrialized countries also need the South's raw materials. Similarly, greater wealth in the poor world should mean a much larger market for the goods produced by the rich world.

Finally, there is now a good deal of evidence to show that much aid, particularly aid directed specifically to the poor, is money well spent, resulting in increased productivity, especially of food.

Opposite An agriculturalist working with farmers in Kenya. Some people feel training and technical assistance are the most valuable forms of aid.

Who benefits?

Aid is a term which covers many different kinds of flow of money, goods and services from the rich world to the poor. Its purpose is generally to promote social and economic development, although some of it may be military, commercial or political in nature and have little to do with the concept of 'aiding the poor'. Indeed, one of the major criticisms levelled against aid is that the political and commercial motives of the rich world in giving it have too often been more important than the real needs of the poor it is given to.

Attitudes to aid Some say that a lot of aid has been wasted. Others go further, claiming that aid has been positively harmful and increased the gap between rich and poor in the Third World, because it has concentrated on the development of urban and industrial sectors. There's a view that aid cannot promote real growth but instead slows it down. It is a substitute for locally-generated growth, increasing poor countries' debts and their dependence on the rich world.

On the whole, however, most poor countries continue to seek and accept aid, seeing it as an essential ingredient in the development process. They limit their debate to how much should be given and under what conditions, rather than whether it should be given at all. They argue for more aid in the form of grants rather than loans, the minimum of strings attached, and a far greater say in deciding how to use it.

Supporters of aid point to its vital role in supplementing a poor country's scarce resources, and providing the first step for what should become self-sustaining economic growth. Few, however, pretend that aid has not had its failures, but they point to encouraging signs of change in both theory and practice.

The trickle-down theory? Perhaps the most important example of a lesson learnt is the shift away from the theory that wealth created at the top of a society would eventually trickle down and benefit the poorest. Before, it was widely believed that aid given to the urban, industrial sector would create the money and incentive for economic growth. The rural areas were expected to provide the food and the labour to fuel this growth, and to share in its benefits as they 'trickled' down. Food prices were often kept artificially low to avoid demands for higher wages by workers in the cities. The result was that poor farmers in the countryside got poorer. The urban middle-class got richer. Peasants were forced to move to the towns in search of work. Food production fell.

> *'Foreign aid is not indispensable to economic progress, and is indeed likely to obstruct it.'*
> Professor Bauer, Dissent on Development

The new philosophy of development turns the trickle-down theory on its head: get money and jobs to the poorest in society, it suggests, develop the rural areas, increase food production, slow the rush to the cities and increase the spending power of the poor, which is more likely to go on locally produced goods – and you may have the beginnings of a viable and self-sustaining economy.

It can be argued that people have expected too much of aid. It is not an exact science. Theories have to be tested and adjusted. Aid may not have worked miracles, but without it the poor would be much worse off. And while the emphasis of aid projects has changed, there remains a place for the large-scale industrial projects funded, for example, by the World Bank. Building a hydroelectric dam may not directly help the poorest, but the development of such a capital-intensive infrastructure is an essential step for a country's overall development, without which it won't make the money to provide the poor with better schools, hospitals or pensions.

'The overwhelming proportion of aid money is usefully spent on the purposes for which it is intended.' *Brandt Report*

Government aid programmes have often been criticised for bypassing the poorest people. Non-governmental agencies, such as Oxfam or Christian Aid, are often able to work at the grassroots more easily. These villagers in Gambia have greatly improved their own water supply through a simple, small-scale well-digging programme run by ActionAid.

Is industry

Although the concentration on industrial development has been blamed for widening the gap between rich and poor, few poor countries want no industry at all. The danger lies more in the kind of industries promoted, and in industrial development which prospers at the expense of the countryside.

> 'If you induce economic growth in a society that is unequal, you will end up with more poor people.'
>
> *Oxfam*

Indeed, most poor countries regard industrialization as a central objective of their development policy. The export of commodities makes up the bulk of the poorer countries' income, but because of their limited industrial capacity they miss out on the money made by processing and the manufacture of próducts based on those commodities. A wider industrial base would enable them to keep a greater share of the profits.

A shoemaker at work, India. In many poor countries, it is small-scale labour-intensive businesses which are most needed. Investment in industries which employ machines rather than people may only increase poverty.

Developing countries want to boost their share of the world's industrial production from 12 per cent (in 1970) to 27 per cent by the year 2000. They argue, however, that rising protectionism, unstable export prices, and increasing costs of the fuel and machinery they need in order to industrialize, all militate against this. Nevertheless, their manufacturing output has been growing twice as fast as that of many already industrialized countries, although this growth has been very uneven. Some countries, such as Brazil, have made tremendous advances; in others, less than 5 per cent of the workforce is engaged in manufacturing.

Producing goods for export? One approach to industrialization is to concentrate on producing exports. This is the model followed by Korea, Taiwan and Singapore, countries often regarded as the South's 'success stories'. Other countries exhibit the dangers of this approach: the wealth generated may not be distributed fairly and the workforce may be exploited, since cheap labour is an important part of their competitiveness in the world market.

The other problem is that export-oriented growth is very vulnerable to changes in world trading conditions. In a recession world markets shrink, and such countries then have greatly reduced incomes with which to pay back the loans which enabled them to industrialize in the first place.

Replacing imports? Countries like Singapore and Hong Kong had to concentrate on export demand because their own home markets were too small for a viable industry. Countries like India, with a large home market and many natural resources, have been able to pursue a different policy. India is now one of the world's leading industrial powers. While she doesn't export a great deal, she is able to meet most of her own needs and has replaced

the key?

many foreign imports with local products. But many smaller countries experience difficulties with this approach, either because their populations don't provide a large enough market, or the majority are too poor to buy much, or they don't have many natural resources to exploit.

Rapid industrialization in the Third World has brought its problems. By diverting government money away from agriculture, it has often led to the decline of rural areas, where most people live. Industrial workers in the Third World are rarely in a position to bargain for better wages and conditions – or pollution control. Many governments have been attracted by capital- rather than labour-intensive projects. Investment funds have gone towards hydroelectric and irrigation schemes, for example, which primarily benefit the urban élite and the bigger landowners, while the poor may lose their land, or suffer adverse environmental effects such as increased waterborne diseases.

There's a great need for small-scale, labour-intensive industries, especially in the rural areas, which would provide jobs and produce products needed locally at a price local people can afford to pay.

A car factory in Brazil, one of the Third World's rapidly industrializing countries. The majority of developing countries are struggling to increase their tiny share of the world's manufacturing industries.

Rural

As people became aware of the limitations of the trickle-down theory (page 32), they started to think instead about working from the 'bottom up', and directing aid to the poorest of all.

In most cases this means aid to the rural areas, not just because increased food production is vital for most poor countries, but also because about 80 per cent of the poorest people in the poor world live there, making their living from the land. Before industrialization can work, it is argued, these people have to have money to spend. It is no good building a toothpaste factory if only a few people in the country can afford to buy toothpaste.

Some argue that money invested in the poor is money wasted because the peasants will only 'eat' it (i.e. spend it on food) rather than

Right Governments need to help the small farmer and improve life for the rural poor if any lasting development is to take place. Can any of the people living here, for example, afford to buy toothpaste?

In most poor countries, the majority of the population live in rural areas. The hard life and lack of facilities are causing increasing numbers to drift to the already overcrowded cities.

'The real power of the future will belong to whoever possesses the source of food.'
Ismail Sabri-Abdullah, Egyptian politician

development

invest it in goods and services. Others disagree, pointing out that rich people in poor countries tend just to buy more consumer goods, often made in the North, while the poor tend to spend their money on better housing, more food and better tools, thus creating demand for small local businesses and crafts.

Helping rural areas? Putting money into agriculture alone is not enough. People are leaving the countryside not just because it is hard to make a living, but because the rural areas have been neglected in every way. Health posts and clinics are few and far between, as are schools. People move to the cities because they feel that, however cramped and squalid their surroundings may be, their children have a better chance of

medical care, education and, eventually, work.

If it is to be worth staying on the land, there have to be far-reaching improvements all round, not just in agriculture. Dividing the land more fairly (land reform) would be part of this.

Increased yields? More of the world's surface could be cultivated, but simply expanding the area under cultivation has sometimes resulted in damage to the environment. Any serious increase in food production is going to have to come from higher yields, yet if these require the use of expensive new technology they can end up worsening the situation of the poorest farmers.

Irrigation can double or even treble yields but it needs careful research and good management. Side-effects have included waterlogged or salty soil, and an increase in waterborne diseases, which sap the energy of the peasant farmer. Often irrigation schemes have ended up benefiting the rich, who then buy up the land of those who could not afford irrigation. So the number of landless families increases. Should poor countries adopt agricultural methods that bring big increases in production if they also increase inequality and landlessness?

Often small family farms can produce more food per hectare than big company ones, yet many peasant farmers lack access to the things which would help them get the best out of the land. Schemes whereby a number of smallholders get reliable seed, fertilizer and advice from a central company which then buys the cash crop they grow for them may seem a step forward, but there can be drawbacks. In many societies, women traditionally produce the family food crops. In some such schemes, they lose the land on which they grew those crops. They become dependent on their husband's cash income to buy food, often from company-controlled shops. This has sometimes led to families receiving less food than they had under the old system.

What kind

Most people in the poor world work on the land. Their countries' economies are largely based on agriculture. Yet they are increasingly unable to feed themselves and depend on the rich world for food. In 1981 they imported more than 100 million tonnes of cereals. Nearly 9 million tonnes of this was supplied as 'food aid'. The rest was bought by poor countries — a bill many can ill afford.

> **'Land where food once grew is now used to grow cotton and peanuts for export.'**
> *Catholic Fund for Overseas Development*

Some say it all began with colonialism. The mother countries used the colonies' land and labour to grow crops they wanted, causing a shift from growing subsistence food crops to a reliance on cash crops. Subsistence crops, such as cassava, millet and other coarse grain and root crops, are grown to feed the farmer's family, with any surplus sold for cash. Cash crops, such as coffee, tobacco or peanuts, are grown entirely for cash, and are usually sold to large commercial companies or through government marketing boards.

Patterns of agriculture Many leaders of the former colonies have made little effort to change this pattern. Indeed, many have concentrated on growing cash crops to earn the foreign exchange they need, and have failed to invest in food production. In order to keep the price of food low and avoid unrest in the cities, they did not pay enough to farmers. As a result, the farmers have been getting poorer and leaving the land, and food production has actually gone down.

The irony is that in order to pay for their food imports, poor countries are using their labour and best land to grow cash crops for the rich world. These are not just things like palm

Right Mechanized large-scale farming in America's mid-west. It produces high yields but may not be the right system for the Third World, where millions of people are dependent for their food and income on farming small plots of land.

# of agriculture?

oil and peanuts, but fruit, flowers, vegetables and beef. This is why some argue that the poor world's problems will not be solved by better prices for their cash crops, but only by a switch from growing cash crops to food crops.

Poor country governments have often been encouraged by western agribusinesses and aid institutions to push cash crop production. And many, even when promoting food rather than cash crops, have apparently been willing to follow western models of food production. Many people regard this as the real issue. Agricultural production can be increased in the poor world; the question is, which kind of system should be followed?

A model food system? The United States has been called the 'bread-basket to end all bread-baskets'. It supplies 64 per cent of the world's total wheat supplies. It is a farming system in which few people actually work the land and a lot of money goes into hybrid seeds, fertilizers, energy and machinery. Farms have had to get larger and larger in order to survive. Small farmers have gone bust. It developed in this way because the US had a lot of fertile land and relatively few people to farm it, and its growing industries were absorbing much of the labour available.

> 'A large and stable agricultural surplus is the first requirement of development.'
> *Paul Harrison,* Inside the Third World

In the poor world, conditions are the reverse, and many argue that agricultural investment there should be directed primarily at the small farmer. The emphasis should be on technology and equipment which makes their labour more productive, rather than replacing it with machinery or promoting dependence on expensive agricultural aids.

How helpful

For more than 25 years massive quantities of food aid have been exported from the West to the Third World to feed the hungry and help development. The Brandt Report called food aid an essential part of the fight to eliminate poverty and hunger, and called for it to be increased. Yet there are many who seriously question its usefulness.

'Using food aid in a carefully planned way multiplies its benefits many times over.'
World Food Programme

A sound recipe for development? The most basic reason to support food aid is that it makes use of a resource that would otherwise be wasted – if the rich have produced too much food and the poor are hungry, why shouldn't the poor benefit? Food aid is often distributed through 'food-for-work' development projects aimed at improving people's living conditions, such as forestry, farming, health or education schemes.

If it is given as payment for work, it makes more development possible since money that would otherwise be used as wages can be put to use elsewhere. Since governments don't

Some people feel 'food-for-work' schemes like this road-building project in India damage local food production. They believe food aid should only be used for famine relief.

is food aid?

pay for most food aid, it promotes development without adding to their debts. It goes directly to those who need it – the poor – because only those willing to exchange their labour for food will receive it.

Food aid can help during seasonal shortages of food, which often reduce people's energies just at the time when the hardest agricultural work has to be done. Food provided at schools or training centres can encourage regular attendance and so help people invest in their futures.

It can also be useful in schemes where old methods of agriculture are being changed or new areas being settled. Food aid can tide people over any transition period when they may be cut off from their traditional food supplies and are not yet able to depend on the new one.

Corruption in the distribution network can be a problem, but food supplies are highly visible and bulky, and can therefore be kept track of more easily than money.

Pitfalls Yet the very bulkiness of food aid means it is enormously expensive to transport. Would that money be better spent, perhaps, helping farmers to grow food themselves more productively? Food can spoil in transport. Not all foods that rich countries make available are acceptable to the recipients. Getting food aid to the right people and places can be a complex process. It may take people with managerial and technical skills away from other development work.

But the main criticism of food aid is that it can damage local food production. It lowers the price of food grown locally, which means poor farmers have less incentive to produce it themselves. So while critics may agree that food aid has some use, they often limit this to emergency famine and refugee relief. Some say the West has used food aid to get rid of awkward surpluses, as a political weapon, and even to prop up undemocratic regimes which they wish to support.

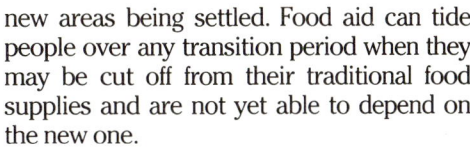

> 'Indiscriminate or uncontrolled use of food aid can do more harm than good.'
> Former Director General, Oxfam

Most seriously, they believe that food aid has relieved politicians of the responsibility for tackling fundamental problems in national food production. Behind most criticisms of food aid lies the Chinese proverb, 'If you give a man a fish, he will live for a day; give him a fishing net and he will live for a lifetime.'

The Green

In the early 1960s, various scientists, economists, government administrators and agriculturalists, supported by aid foundations and agribusinesses, worked out a series of techniques which would lead to greater agricultural production.

The whole package became known as the Green Revolution. It involved the introduction of improved seeds which, given plenty of fertilizer, pesticides, reliable irrigation and drainage, produce very high-yielding plants. Harvests improved dramatically. Food production went up. Even though farming with the new seeds was more costly, the higher incomes compensated.

Growing pains A decade later, some worrying side-effects became apparent. The new 'miracle' seeds were more uniform and so much more vulnerable to attack by insects or disease. In the past, one area might contain many different strains of wheat or rice, not all of which would suffer from the same kinds of blights. After the Green Revolution, a mere handful of varieties can make up the bulk of a country's harvest. This is not only the poor world's problem. In 1970, southern corn-leaf blight had a disastrous effect on the American corn crop.

Because the big seed companies find it more profitable to limit the varieties available to the consumer, this problem is increasing. The breeding, collection and conservation of the world's seed varieties is largely in the hands of the rich world, although the majority of the collection comes originally from the South, who thus find yet another of their natural resources under the control of the North.

More food = less hunger? Its critics allege that the Green Revolution may have produced more food, but not fewer hungry people. The benefits have gone mainly to the richer farmers, who could afford the initial outlay needed. As yields went up, land became more valuable. Poor farmers found themselves being bought out by their rich neighbours. The

The Green Revolution dramatically increased yields for those farmers who could afford the new seeds and fertilizer, as here in the Andes. However, it also increased the gap between them and their poorer neighbours.

Revolution

number of poor, landless peasants increased. The Green Revolution may not have created these inequalities but it did exaggerate them.

Many of the elements which make up the Green Revolution package are manufactured by the transnational seed companies. Thus the Green Revolution has also meant big business for large corporations, usually based in the rich world.

Yet, however much people criticise some effects of the Green Revolution, there is always the answer that, although a flawed step forward, it was ultimately a very valuable one. As Indian Prime Minister Mrs Gandhi explained, what has to be done now is to find ways of dealing with the flaws: 'Our Green Revolution was absolutely essential for our survival.

> **'Give us this day our daily bread should not become a prayer to Shell Oil.'** *Third World diplomat*

There is no doubt that it put India on its feet. At the same time it increased the gap. It helped the richer farmer more than the man who irrigated the land . . . What we now need to do is help the smaller farmer.'

The solution is not necessarily to abandon the new agricultural technology, but to encourage even more sophisticated research which will benefit the poorest farmer. It is a much greater challenge to develop seeds which can flourish on difficult land and under unstable conditions.

Research into seed varieties which would flourish in the difficult conditions faced by these farmers in Upper Volta, for example, would be of real benefit to the poorest people.

A price for progress?

Development is not without its hidden dangers. There is the difficulty of ensuring that the benefits actually reach those they are meant to. And there is the problem of predicting any possible side-effects and balancing them against the gains. And while it is generally recognized that development can rarely be painless, some people claim that the unwelcome social and economic changes it brings are all too often the result of inadequate research and planning, and a lack of will to see that those who benefit really are the poorest.

Weighing the benefits When a new road is built in the mountainous Himalayan foothills of Nepal, where the majority of the population eke out a living from steeply terraced fields, it may reduce a four-day trek to a four-hour bus ride. Formerly everything – from bags of seeds and fertilizer to tin roofing sheets – had to be carried on people's backs up rocky trails. But back-breaking as such portering is, it was one of the few sources of paid work for the poorest villagers. Thus, the new road can actually make things worse for them.

Governments and aid agencies increasingly recognize that such 'improvements' have to be part of a wider package. The road construction needs to be backed up by efforts to start other resources of employment, to increase food production, and to improve village health and education facilities.

Tourism Some poor countries don't have much choice over their route to development. For example, countries with few or no exportable commodities may see their climate and geographical features as one of the few natural resources they can exploit.

Tourism earns foreign exchange. It provides jobs, both directly in hotels, for example, and indirectly for taxi drivers, souvenir sellers, guides and others. It can increase people's respect for and understanding of different cultures. It can encourage the revival or preservation of traditional crafts and cultural traditions. It may lead to infrastructure building, such as roads, water supplies and airports. It provides a welcome alternative income for countries with a single-crop economy.

Yet much of the food tourists eat is imported from the rich world. The profits from their package holiday usually stay in their own country. Holiday companies and hotels sometimes negotiate exemption from certain taxes before investing in a Third World country. Tourists don't want to take risks, and income can fall dramatically if tour operators sense any social unrest.

Wages for those who work in tourism are often low, and the work itself is usually seasonal. The beginning of the tourist season sometimes coincides with the harvest and so draws valuable labour away from the rural areas. Local children may skip school for a day to beg or act as guides, and earn as much as a peasant farmer can earn in a week. The disparity between the wealth of tourists and the local population can cause discontent and confusion. Are these disadvantages balanced by the money tourism brings in?

Solutions to development issues are rarely clearcut. Building a road to this man's village in Nepal may bring some obvious benefits; but for him and other poor villagers, it will mean the loss of their only form of employment – portering.

'There are hardly any large-scale dams, hydroelectric or irrigation schemes in the world which have not caused substantial and usually avoidable damage.'
Jon Tinker, Earthscan

Appropriate

As economic change takes place in the poor world and the use of technology increases, the nature and role of that technology is becoming an issue of great concern. Many feel that not enough time or money has been spent in searching for technology which is right for the Third World, and not a mere imitation of what is done in the West.

One of the most obvious examples of this is the introduction of industries based on expensive machinery in countries where labour is plentiful and money is not – for example, building a plastic shoe factory which provides 40 jobs, but puts hundreds of shoemakers and their suppliers out of work.

dominance. However, it is generally accepted that an emphasis on appropriate technology is a good thing, and means not the adoption of less recent or less sophisticated technology, but rather that which is best suited to local incomes, objectives and conditions.

Small is beautiful? Appropriate technology can include cheaper sources of energy, simpler farm equipment which doesn't require expensive and scarce spare parts, or building techniques which make full use of local materials. A large number of small-scale, widely dispersed operations, which are cheap to set up and can reach more people, are better than

> ## 'It is machinery that has impoverished India.'
> *Mahatma Gandhi*

To imitate or not to imitate? Advertising and other marketing techniques often encourage the use of modern aids which are inappropriate to the poor's lifestyle.

This is graphically illustrated by baby food companies' aggressive marketing of breast-milk substitutes in the Third World. Poor women often lack access to either clean water or enough fuel regularly to boil water and sterilize bottles. Consequently they dilute the expensive milk-powder or mix it with impure water in order to give their babies what they have been persuaded is so much better for them than breastmilk. All too often babies become ill or malnourished, and are actually worse off than they would have been if breastfed.

There is a decline in the earlier enthusiasm, on the part of both rich and poor, for the straightforward transfer of technology from one to the other. Yet this in turn has aroused suspicions among some people in the poor world, who fear a conspiracy to fob them off with second-rate or backward technology so that the rich world can keep its technological

answers?

a few large ones complete with the latest equipment.

Commercial companies control most technological developments, and are perhaps unlikely to finance research which does not promise much profit. Yet the North will also benefit from less wasteful, more appropriate technology, for it is the resources of the whole world (wood, oil, etc.) which are being used up.

Of course, certain processes are better done on a large scale. Equally, not every industry benefits from being labour-intensive. And poor people do benefit from technology which makes time-consuming, repetitive tasks easier. But the important thing is that the technology enables them to be more productive, rather than depriving them of a job altogether.

The same principle applies in medical and educational systems. When health care is concentrated in the cities of a poor country, and the vast majority of the population live in the countryside, the system is clearly inappropriate. But as long as the rural areas remain neglected, it will be hard to attract doctors and nurses to work there. Giving a few villagers a basic training in healthcare – 'the barefoot doctor' idea which has been successfully pioneered in China – would seem the more appropriate answer.

75% of the diseases are in the countryside and 75% of the doctors are in the towns.' WHO

Chinese barefoot doctors, with their simple training and the minimum of equipment, can bring basic medical care within reach of far more people than if the same amount of money had been spent on modern hospitals and highly-trained doctors.

The role

It is generally agreed that people are a country's greatest resource. The rate and quality of its development is ultimately determined by them, rather than by its financial or natural resources.

Many poor countries feel their development is held back by a shortage of trained people (eg. doctors, teachers and engineers), so a good education system has always been high on their list of priorities. Lee Kuan Yew, President of Singapore, attributes much of his country's impressive economic development to the importance the government attached to training technicians, engineers and managers.

Yet rapid expansion of education systems, which has been absorbing a large proportion of many poor countries' limited funds, has not always led to correspondingly rapid development. Some have blamed the inherited colonial education systems which encouraged higher education for the few rather than basic education for the majority. Yet many Third World governments, with some notable exceptions such as Tanzania, have concentrated on simply expanding these education systems, rather than changing them.

Education for what? The many bitter, unemployed graduates in India, Sri Lanka and elsewhere, who cannot get the jobs they are qualified for, bear witness to the problems created by inappropriate education. Some Third World ministries of education have been criticised for putting too much stress on education for jobs in modern industries and cities. They produce students whose hopes are unrealistic and often unfulfilled, yet who have become alienated from the rural areas, which need their skills most.

Another way in which scarce resources may be wasted is by trained people leaving poor countries to work in the rich world. Some say that everyone benefits from this 'brain drain': the North from their skills and the South from the high wages they send home. But ultimately this represents a great loss of the skilled manpower which poor countries so badly need.

Agriculture is on the curriculum of this school in Lesotho, southern Africa. Education needs to be more relevant to the lives of the poor if it is to help them become properly self-reliant.

# of education?

Education for life? This is not to say that education should not remain a priority. Without education, the poor are at the mercy of those, such as landowners or moneylenders, who may wish to exploit their illiteracy. They can be cheated, forced to sign away their rights to land, are hampered in political knowledge and action, and have little chance of improving their lifestyles by getting a better job. 'Literacy – which goes beyond being able to read and write – arouses people's consciousness and helps them participate in community life. Thus it is also a prerequisite for fighting hunger and disease,' said the Brandt Report.

One of the problems education faces in poor countries is the very high drop-out rate. This is often because a child's labour is badly needed to supplement the family's income, and because the education being received can seem of little relevance. Teachers are often

> *'Schools have been potent instruments of westernization among the young . . . [they] emerge dazed and uprooted, despising their own culture.'* Paul Harrison, Inside the Third World

badly trained, paid and supervised, because those best qualified are rarely attracted to work in the rural areas. The teaching may be done in the national language, as opposed to the local or regional language spoken by most of the pupils, and is only of use to the very few pupils who may go on to further education or to work in the town or for the government.

If education is really to help the poorest, it has to be made more practical, and more immediately relevant to their life.

The poor world is also poor in its means of communication and information. It lacks access not only to books, but to the whole range of information technology which assists social and economic planning.

'At least 50 per cent of world food is produced by women. In some parts of Africa this rises to 90 per cent.'

UNICEF

Women have not always been helped by economic development. In many countries they produce the family's food and sell the surplus at market. Yet, as development schemes direct farming and marketing advice to men alone, women can find themselves losing out.

the family?

While economists and politicians debate debt crises and commodity prices at the international level, how have things improved at the family level?

It has been said that the family is the basis of society. And if you look at the family, you must look at women, who generally provide family care. More than a quarter of all households in the world are headed by women, with the percentage much higher in certain regions where, for example, men are forced to find work away from home. These households are among the poorest of the poor.

The fate of women Among the poor, it is usually women who suffer most. They are often the last to be fed and gain the least nourishment, even though pregnancy and childcare means their need is greater. As well as cooking and looking after the home and children, they often do as much as – and sometimes more than – 50 per cent of the farm work. They traditionally have the time-consuming tasks of fetching water and firewood, and processing the crops (winnowing rice, shelling groundnuts etc.), while men's work tends to be that assisted by animals or machinery, for example ploughing.

While improvements to water supplies, health and family planning services have undoubtedly helped women, many feel that they are all too often overlooked, and sometimes their situation made worse, by the development process.

For better or for worse? Governments' policies of keeping down food prices in the cities has meant low prices for the crops women cultivate. When land reform takes place, ownership of land usually goes to men. If women do manage to own land, they find agricultural advice, technological improvements and other help is largely directed towards men. And mechanization of men's work can add to the women's workload by increasing, for example, the amount of weeding and food processing required.

Industrialization has often meant that petty trading and traditional crafts have died out, both of which are sources of income for women. Women working in the new industries are frequently lower paid than men. New agricultural schemes have also sometimes made things worse for women, as they have exchanged their control over the family's food supply, which they grew, for dependence on their husband's wage packet with which to buy food.

Women have also been a major target for advertising campaigns which persuade them to buy 'modern' goods which may well be inappropriate and waste precious money. They have not profited from the expanded educational facilities as much as men, sometimes because of discrimination, but also because, from an early age, girls are expected to take on a large slice of a family's domestic and farming work. Of the world's population who are illiterate, 60 per cent are women. In some countries this figure rises to 80 per cent and even higher.

Any development, however carefully planned, involves social change and a difficult shift between the old and the new. There is generally an 'in-between' period when the old private support systems, such as the extended family, are breaking up, but the new public ones, supplied by the state, are not yet able to replace them. Not surprisingly, the burden of this period tends to fall on women, particularly those with the dual responsibility of keeping a family and a job.

'Overlooked or even displaced by the development process, women neither participate in it nor benefit from its results.'
UNFPA

> '*Because of deforestation, by the year 2000 India could have enough food but not enough fuel to cook it.*'
> Sumi Krishna Chauhan, journalist

The industrial world's energy consumption far outstrips that of the poor world. And within the poor world, too, schemes tend to benefit the relatively well-off.

Here in India, beneath the high-voltage electricity pylons, dung is being dried out in flat cakes before being burned. It is the only fuel these people can afford.

Equal in energy?

Energy is a central issue in the debate between rich and poor: who owns it, who sells it and for how much, and who consumes it. Energy is vital to the exploitation of all other resources. Lack of it will cause any economy – rich or poor – to fail.

Cheap coal fuelled the growth of the Industrial Revolution. Cheap oil was vital to the way the rich world has, since the Second World War, raised its standard of living. The poor world did not benefit in the same way then, but it did suffer when the oil-fed boom in the rich world came to an end. The demand for raw materials slackened, commodity prices dropped, and the incomes of the poor world fell sharply. Much of the oil was in the hands of a group of countries which, although they could hardly now be described as poor, were identified with the South rather than with the rich industrialized North.

The wood crisis Third World countries without their own sources of energy have been hard hit by the rise in the price of oil, which they need for industrialization and development. However, the energy crisis which faces most people in the Third World is not one of rising gas or electricity bills, but of dwindling supplies of wood. Nine out of ten people in the poor world rely on wood as their chief source of energy. In some areas, collecting enough fuel can take women several hours each day. And when firewood is in short supply, people burn animal dung. Thus their precious natural fertilizer, which should be enriching their fields, goes up in smoke.

Deterioration of the environment affects both rich and poor countries, and the gradual depletion of the world's forests is bad news for everyone. Quicker-growing trees are helping to meet some of the demand for fuel and animal fodder which is causing the deforestation, but it remains a slow process. Research is being done into alternative forms of energy, such as solar and wind power, gas made from animal, human and vegetable waste, and other renewable sources, but as yet without any great impact on the energy gap.

Consumption and supply Meanwhile the world is using up its finite resources at a dramatic rate. And it is the rich world which is the main consumer. North America, with 6 per cent of the world's population, consumes more than 33 per cent of its energy. Western Europe uses 20 per cent, Latin America 4 per cent, and Africa only 2 per cent. No amount of alternative energy is going to be developed fast enough to meet the demands of the industrialized world.

Nuclear energy is one highly controversial way proposed to resolve the energy crisis. Those who support it argue that it is the cheapest large-scale, long-term way of producing electricity. They believe the dangers of not developing nuclear power are greater than the risks, because a world in which the oil has run out will be neither stable nor peaceful. Their opponents believe the world would do better to consume less energy, and concentrate on developing less potentially lethal energy sources.

> '*All the fuel used by the Third World is only slightly more than the gasoline the North burns to move its automobiles.*'
> Brandt Report

Food

'Developing countries now spend more money on arms than they spend on health and education put together.' *Christian Aid*

or guns?

Local people in the Ogaden being trained to use the latest military hardware. Throughout the conflict in the Horn of Africa, huge sums of money have changed hands in arms deals while millions of people are starving and homeless.

The introduction to the Brandt Report asked: 'Could one be content to call something a new world economic order if it did not include major progress towards disarmament?' It gives a number of examples of the sort of money that is currently being spent on arms, and puts this into perspective by showing what the same amount of money could do if used for development. For example, for the price of one jet fighter ($20 million), about 40,000 village pharmacies could be set up. The world's military expenditure of only half a day would finance the World Health Organization's entire malaria eradication programme.

The arms trade Unrest and civil war in the South have caused many Third World governments to believe that spending money on armed forces and weapons is the best way to protect their interests. This, coupled with the rich world's willingness to make money by supplying them with arms, has led to a very steep rise in military spending by the poor world. The main suppliers of arms to the world are the USA, the USSR, France, Britain and West Germany. 'It is a terrible irony that the most dynamic and rapid transfer of highly sophisticated equipment and technology from rich to poor countries has been in the machinery of death,' says the Brandt Report.

> 'Half the world's population lack clean water and adequate sanitation. To provide them would cost ¹/₂₀th of what the world currently spends on arms.' *Catholic Fund for Overseas Development*

The world spends far more on arms than on development, but it is not just a question of money. Manpower and skills are currently devoted to perfecting ever more efficient and sophisticated weapons. These could be diverted into much more productive research:

the prevention of debilitating diseases, for example, or increases in agricultural production. But a malaria vaccine, whose main customers would be the world's poorest people, does not offer the same profit margin as a machine gun.

There is, of course, a more direct way in which people suffer as a result of military spending. Since the end of the Second World War there have been well over a hundred local wars. Millions of people have been killed, wounded or forced to become refugees. The death and misery resulting from the use of arms is immeasurable.

Alternative approaches Most people who believe in disarmament are working to prevent the spread of nuclear weapons and any possibility of nuclear war. But 80 per cent of the world's military spending actually goes on 'ordinary' weapons, i.e. non-nuclear ones. Some experts have proposed a tax on the arms trade. The money raised could be used specifically for development purposes, and would provide funds on an automatic and predictable basis which would make development planning much easier.

Another lobby feels that education has a key role to play. They believe in increasing people's awareness that the world's survival does not depend on maintaining balances of military power, but on international efforts to protect and preserve the biological environment and ensure the equal sharing of its resources. No world, they say, can be a safe or peaceful one when the majority of its population are poor and malnourished.

Arms spending makes the world poorer, not safer. It aggravates the causes of war by absorbing money which could otherwise be used to tackle poverty, disease, unemployment and the other social ills which worry people and pressure them into feeling they must protect their own interests — by force if necessary.

A question

Many of us as children suffered the fate of staring glumly at the remains of some fatty stew or stodgy pudding, unable to finish it, and being told to think of the starving millions and eat it all up. You may well have wondered how finishing your food could possibly help a starving child thousands of miles away. Yet there is a growing feeling in the rich world that ordinary people can help to narrow the gap between them and the poor world by changes in their lifestyles.

Who consumes what? When people talk about pressure on the world's resources, they often cite population growth in poor countries as the greatest threat. The world, they say, has to maintain the correct balance between the resources we have and the number of people who consume them. Too many people and the equation collapses. Others feel the equation is more complicated than that, because some people use up resources at a much faster rate than others. For example, rich countries contain 25 per cent of the world's population yet consume about 66 per cent of the world's food. Their animals alone eat 30 per cent of the world's grain.

It is the same story with energy. The indus-

While millions lack an adequate diet, some 30 per cent of the world's grain is being fed to livestock in the rich world. It can take 10 kilos of grain to produce one kilo of steak.

# of lifestyles?

trialized countries as a whole use up 85 per cent of the world's oil. The average North American uses as much energy as 53 Indians, 109 Sri Lankans and 1,072 Nepalese. The North's consumption of commercial energy doubled between 1960 and 1976. In the same period consumption in developing countries tripled, but it was still only $\frac{1}{15}$th of what the West was consuming.

While industry in the North accounts for much of the energy use, oil's relative cheapness until the early 1970s also allowed westerners to develop a way of life which is highly energy-intensive and often wasteful. The 'oil

crisis' did alert people to the need to save energy, but much more could still be done.

Some western eating habits, too, are especially wasteful in global terms. Someone in the West may well eat five times as much grain as a poor person, 90 per cent of it via meat and dairy products from animals who have themselves been fed on grain. It can take up to ten kilos of grain to produce one kilo of meat or dairy produce. Experts have estimated that a reduction of only 10 per cent in the amount of meat Americans eat would release enough grain to feed 60 million people – and at the same time reduce the number of heart attacks in the USA.

Problems and alternatives But while reduced demand for feed grain might affect the amount of grain available for human consumption, availability by itself is not enough. If the extra grain is to reach the poor, it must be sold at a price they can afford. Yet if the price of grain consistently drops, farmers are likely to cut their production. And some Third World countries which rely on exporting beef, such as Argentina, would suffer from a reduction in meat consumption.

> **'In the end, solutions come from individual people doing something different.'** UNEP

In spite of the difficulties involved in turning changes in the rich world's lifestyle into positive benefits for the poor, there has undoubtedly been a growing disenchantment with the western idea of growth for growth's sake. People have been looking for alternative lifestyles and greater spiritual development. There are those who believe that real world change stems from the decisions of individuals, not governments, and that only when enough people change their personal values and ideals can the gap between rich and poor worlds begin truly to be closed.

The

Negotiations over the New International Economic Order (page 18) are felt by many to have reached stalemate. People have lost some of their enthusiasm for aid as a means of promoting development. There are more undernourished, under-employed and badly housed people in the world than ever before.

If all the discussion and the action taken have failed greatly to change the situation of the poor, is it because people lack the means to change things – or the will? Is it because the kind of development the poor world has been striving for and the rich world has endorsed is the wrong model? Or is it because the idea of a just world, in which hunger and poverty no longer exist, is an impossible dream?

A political solution? Some argue that the solution is purely political, and should be based on one or a mixture of the world's main systems, such as communism, socialism or free-market capitalism.

> 'We need not more of the same, but something different and that is the heart of the matter between North and South today.'
> Shridath Ramphal, Commonwealth Secretary-General

Yet the variety of religious, cultural and historical traditions which exist in developing countries, as well as the differences in climate, terrain and available resources, make it hard to put forward any single blueprint or plan for development. China and South Korea, although poles apart in ideology, have both made considerable progress economically. Many other developing countries would find their respective approaches neither suitable nor acceptable.

One guideline may be that any system needs to fit closely with and draw strength from existing traditions and principles in that society.

Shortsighted view? Others say any improvements really depend on the ability of the North to stop seeing the development of the South as a threat, and to start recognizing that it is in everyone's interest – rich and poor – that the world's economy is strengthened, that its resources are better managed and conserved, and that poverty and hunger are eliminated. They do not pretend that the restructuring of the present economic order will be painless for the North, but they stress that the gains far outweigh the costs.

Others argue that the stumbling block to real progress lies not just in the North's shortsightedness, but also in its lack of political will. Politicians act on short-term policies

next step?

because they want to be re-elected. Until the people who elect the politicians really want changes in the international economic order, their leaders will do little.

A change of attitudes? The increasing numbers of small political pressure groups, especially those concerned with protecting the environment, may be the first signs that westerners are beginning to question the values by which they have been living. There is a growing feeling that the world is shared by everyone, in both rich and poor countries, and that nations need to work together to look after it.

There is also growing support for the belief that, in the Third World, poor people, rather than just their governments, must have a greater say in the development process.

Related to this is the idea that the way to achieve a better world is not to create more and more wealth, but to change people's outlook. Instead of seeing progress as the development of more and more products, we should see it, perhaps, as the development of people and their potential.

The issues raised in this book may seem hard to resolve, but that is no reason not to search honestly for an answer. As one writer put it: 'How can we transcend the fear that there are perhaps no answers? Not with self-deception but with honest hope' (Frances More Lappé).

> 'The health of our planet depends on the smooth function of every part, not merely the opulence of a few.'
>
> *Peter Ustinov, UNICEF Goodwill Ambassador*

Working together – the only way to close the gap between rich and poor, and become one world?

Reference

Glossary

Aid – The flow of resources from richer to poorer countries. Types of aid include *financial aid*, either in the form of a loan, which has to be paid back, or in the form of a grant, which is a gift; *tied aid*, which has to be spent by the country receiving it on goods and/or services provided by the donor country; and *technical cooperation*, which is the transfer of skills, advice and information, for example educating and training people, providing consultancies and scientific research.

Official aid has two channels: *bilateral aid* which goes directly from country to country (59% of Britain's aid is bilateral); and *multilateral aid*, administered by organizations which get their resources from more than one country (for example, the World Health Organization).

Aid is also dispersed through *non-governmental organizations*, sometimes called voluntary agencies. These collect funds from the public to undertake development work, disaster relief, research and/or educational work about the Third World.

Capital-intensive industry – One which is based on putting a lot of money into machinery and using relatively little labour.

Cash crops – Crops such as tea, cotton or peanuts grown entirely for cash and usually sold to commercial companies or through government marketing schemes.

Common Fund – A fund agreed at UNCTAD to provide the money to stabilize commodity prices and what developing countries earn from them.

Infrastructure – Goods and services, such as roads, electricity systems, health and medical services, which allow a country to function and be productive.

Labour-intensive industry – One which makes much use of labour and requires a relatively small investment in machinery.

New International Economic Order (NIEO) – A programme of radical changes in the world economy in the interests of developing countries, first discussed in the 1970s.

North/South dialogue – The continuing negotiations between developing and industrialized countries about the NIEO.

Stabex – An EEC scheme to compensate certain countries for falls in their export earnings from the sale of commodities.

Useful addresses

The array of materials on world development and the North/South dialogue is extensive and can seem bewildering. Good places **to start** include:

The Centre for World Development Education (CWDE), 128 Buckingham Palace Road, London SW1W 9SH (Tel: 01-730 8332/3)
Its main aim is to promote education in Britain about world development issues and Britain's interdependence with the Third World. It produces its own publications and is a resource centre for materials from a wide range of other sources. A catalogue is available which gives helpful descriptions of all the books, pamphlets, games, posters, and slide and photo-sets available.

Third World Publications, 151 Stratford Road, Birmingham B11 1RD (Tel: 021 773 6572)
A non-profit-making organization which distributes books from and about the Third World. A catalogue is available.

*Another good place for **resources** (to buy or hire) and for information on local activities and meetings is your local Development Education Centre. To find your nearest one, contact:

National Association of Development Education Centres, 128 Buckingham Palace Road, London SW1W 9SH (Tel: 01-730 0972)

Scottish Education and Action for Development, 29 Nicolson Square, Edinburgh EH8 9BX (Tel: 031 667 0120)

Welsh Centre for International Affairs, Temple of Peace, Cathays Park, Cardiff CF1 3AP (Tel: 0222 28549/395664)

World Development Group, 6 Shipquay Street, Derry, Northern Ireland BT48 6DN (Tel: 0504 69183)

*The following organizations produce **educational materials** on their work, and the broader issues of world development and interdependence:

ActionAid, PO Box 69, 208 Upper Street, London N1 1RZ (Tel: 01-226 3383)

Christian Aid, PO Box 1, London SW9 8BM (Tel: 01-733 5500)

Catholic Fund for Overseas Development, 2 Garden Close, Stockwell Road, London SW9 9TY (Tel: 01-735 9041)

Commonwealth Institute, Kensington High Street, London W8 6NQ (Tel: 01-603 4535)

International Planned Parenthood Federation, 18-20 Lower Regent Street, London SW1 (Tel: 01-839 2911)

Oxfam, Education Department, 274 Banbury Road, Oxford OX2 7DX (Tel: 0865 56777)

Population Concern, Margaret Pyke Street, London W1N 7RJ (Tel: 01-637 9582)

UNICEF UK, 55-56 Lincoln's Inn Fields, London WC2A 3NB (Tel: 01-405 5592)

War on Want, 467 Caledonian Road, London N7 9BE (Tel: 01-690 0211)

World Development Movement, 26 Bedford Chambers, London WC2 E8A (Tel: 01-836 3672)

Earthscan, 10 Percy Street, London W1P 0DR (Tel: 01-580 7574)

Intermediate Technology Development Group, 9 King Street, London WC2E 8HN (Tel: 01-836 9434/9)

United Nations Information Centre, 14-15 Stratford Place, London W1N 9AF (Tel: 01-630 1981)

Overseas Development Administration, Information Department, Eland House, Stag Place, London SW1E 5DH (Tel: 01-213 4853)
The information department has free publications on the British aid programme and development issues. It publishes an extremely useful guide 'Overseas development and aid: A guide to sources of information and material'.

World Studies Project of the One World Trust, 24 Palace Chambers, Bridge Street, London SW1A 2JT (Tel: 01-930 7661)
The Project's publications and activities are aimed towards secondary schools and cover world development, the world environment, human rights, conflicts and war. A publication list is available.

Useful resources

World Development Report (World Bank)
Published each year, this contains detailed information on the world economy and points up long-term trends and prospects. It includes tables and other graphic aids.

The Development Puzzle (Centre for World Development Education/Hodder and Stoughton Educational)
Provides a clear introduction to development topics, illustrated with cartoons, photographs and diagrams, plus an extensive resources guide.

Cartoon Sheet Discussion Starters (Centre for World Development Education)
Basic facts and general explanation of the issues and problems which make up the North/South dialogue, presented in 14 six-sided leaflets. Illustrated with black and white photographs, cartoons and graphics, the leaflets cover trade, unemployment, water, food and agriculture, the least developed countries, energy, population, health, aid, education, environment, disarmament, children and women.

Commodity Sheet Discussion Starters (Centre for World Development Education)
These are useful introductions to any debate on world interdependence and the special difficulties of developing countries in world trade. The first nine titles cover jute, coffee, rice, wheat, maize, tea, copper, bananas and tin.

Facing Up to Change: Britain and the Brandt Report (Centre for World Development Education)
Lively cassette tape/slide discussion starter with script and helpful notes. It can be hired for a small fee.

The Rich and the Poor (Ely Resources and Technology Centre)
An imaginative pack of 100 playing cards which can be used for a variety of games. The pack includes notes on ways to use them and was devised specifically for secondary schools.

Change and Choice: Britain in an Interdependent World (Centre for World Development Education)
This pack contains five case studies, with wallcharts, on interdependence in a British school, a British town, a multinational company, the textile industry and a Sri Lankan village. There are five discussion papers on environment, trade, investment, food and health, 18 illustrated factsheets and a teachers' booklet. Parts of the pack can be bought separately.

Interdependence (Jordanhill Project in International Understanding, Glasgow)
A pack containing a collection of illustrated material developed for 15-16 year olds doing Modern Studies.

(All the above publications are available from the Centre for World Development Education.)

The Creation of World Poverty by Teresa Hayter (Pluto Press, 1981)
An alternative view of the Brandt Report.

Inside the Third World by Paul Harrison (Pelican, 2nd edition 1981)
A comprehensive look at the realities of life for poor people and their communities.

The Third World Tomorrow by Paul Harrison (Pelican, 1980)
First-hand and very readable reports of how concepts such as self-help, cooperatives and small-scale appropriate technology are being put into practice in Africa, Asia and Latin America.

Inside the Inner City by Paul Harrison (Pelican, 1983)
The author relates poverty in Hackney, east London, to poverty worldwide.

Rich World, Poor World by Geoffrey Lean (George Allen and Unwin, 1978)
Provides a very clear and easy to read introduction to the problems of development and the gulf between rich and poor.

World Bank Atlas (World Bank)
Published every year, and available from the Overseas Development Administration, this contains the most up-to-date figures worldwide for GNP, population and growth rates.

The New State of the World Atlas (Pan, 1984)
Can be used as an alternative or complement to the *World Bank Atlas* since it presents, in maps and figures, the facts about worldwide issues such as mineral and food power, pollution, science, law and order, military and state expenditure, and interdependence.

Population Misconceptions (Population Concern, 1984)
Highlights some of the popular misconceptions about population, development and family planning.

Index

Numbers in **bold** refer to illustrations and captions

Credits

The author and publishers would like to thank the following for their kind permission to reproduce copyright illustrations:

Action Aid: 32–3
Camera Press Ltd: 6, 15, 20, 22, 23
Daily Telegraph Colour Library: cover
Mark Edwards/Earthscan: 5, 18–19, 36 (top), 45, 52–3
FAO: 14, 40–41, 42, 43
Sally and Richard Greenhill: 4, 7, 38–9, 46, 56–7
Sunil Gupta/Action Aid: 34
Mansell Collection: 10
Rex Features Ltd: 21, 28–9, 35, 50, 54
Save the Children Fund: 12–13 (photo Mike Wells), 48 (photo Penny Tweedie), 58–9 (photo Mike Wells)
South American Pictures/Tony Morrison: 27
Liba Taylor: 30
UN: 25, 49
Werner Forman Archive/British Museum: 11
Philip Wolmuth: 8, 17, 24, 36–7 (bottom)

Picture research by Suzanne Williams; design by Norman Reynolds.